Forty Days

in the Covid Wilderness
Meditations of Hope

Rev. Dr. Embra Jackson Jr.

Senior Pastor of First United Methodist Church Tupelo, Mississippi

Copyright © 2022 Rev. Dr. Embra Jackson Jr.

Cover Photo Credit: Shannon Turner.

Back Cover Photo Credit: Tom Wicker

Song "Though It All" by Andre Crouch © 1971, renewed 1999 by Manna Music, Inc.

All rights reserved. No part of this publication may be reproduced, distributed, or transmitted in any form or by any means, including photocopying, recording, or other electronic or mechanical methods, without the prior written permission of the publisher, except in the case of brief quotations embodied in critical reviews and certain other noncommercial uses permitted by copyright law.

Scripture quotations are taken from the **New Revised Standard Version Updated Edition**. Copyright © 2021 National Council of Churches of Christ in the United States of America. Used by permission. All rights reserved worldwide.

ISBN: 978-1-951300-48-7

Liberation's Publishing ~ West Point MS. 39773

Forty Days

in the Covid Wilderness
Meditations of Hope

Table of Contents

Acknowledgements vii

Introduction ix

Day 1 1

Day 2 3

Day 3 5

Day 4 7

Day 5 9

Day 6 10

Day 7 13

Day 8 15

Day 9 17

Day 10 19

Day 11 20

Day 12 22

Day 13 24

Day 14 27

Day 15 28

Day 16 30

Day 17 32

Day 18 34

Day 19 36

Day 20 39

Day 21 40

Day 22 42

Day 23 45

Day 24 46

Day 25 49

Day 26 50

Day 27 52

Day 28 54

Day 29 56

Day 30 58

Day 31 60

Day 32 63

Day 33 65

Day 34 67

Day 35 69

Day 36 71

Day 37 72

Day 38 75

Day 39 77

Day 40 78

About The Author 81

Acknowledgements

I would like to begin by thanking God for loving me in spite of my human frailties. I wish to thank Bishop James Swanson for appointing me to First United Methodist Church, Tupelo, Mississippi. Where the laity serve in order to help us fulfill our vision statement: "Experience God's Love; Grow in Christ and Serve All People." Also, I must acknowledge my foreparts, my father Embra Knox Jackson, Sr., and my mother, Allie (Foster) Jackson, who are responsible for my existence. Others include my brother, Lee Walter Payne, Jr. and my mother-in-law, Christine Ousley Gore. All of these now rest from their labors with the Lord. In addition, I acknowledge my beautiful wife, Rosia, who inspires me to be the best I can be each day. To our children: Embra III, Ebony, Emmanuel and Katelyn, I am thankful for your love and support.

The inspiration for this book came from my church members of First United Methodist Church, Tupelo, especially Dr. Joe Edd Morris. Joe Edd is a retired United Methodist Pastor, a psychologist, and a renowned author. Rosia and I have read and enjoyed some of his fictional works. His non-fictional work, *Ten Things I Wish Jesus Hadn't Said* I have found helpful in research and sermon preparation, along with two books co-authored by another member of our church, Dr. Roy H. Ryan—*Old Testament Stories: What Do They Say Today?* and its companion volume, *New Testament Stories: What Do They Say Today?* Joe Edd's wife, Sandi, also edited this book. Thanks to Shannon Turner, our church administrator, who spent countless hours uploading and transcribing the devotions. He and Tom Wicker, another member, are responsible for the book's cover photos. Words of gratitude to Nicole Mangum of Liberation's Publishing for shepherding this book through the publishing process.

Rev. Dr. Embra Jackson Jr.

Introduction

Lent is a time of the wilderness. It is 40 days of reflection on the last 40 days of Jesus 'earthly life that begins with Him being driven by the Spirit into the desert. In the desert, Jesus was tempted for 40 days. Lent is also a reminder of the Israelites wondering in the desert for 40 years. In our traveling through the desert, we often discover things about ourselves and our relationship with God. The idea for this devotion book came from my dear friend and church member, Dr. Joe Edd Morris. He stated that the devotions I had shared with our congregation during the early days of the pandemic (2020-2021) were meaningful to many people who were struggling with the isolation and fear brought on by the pandemic. I recorded these devotions using my cellphone, and then the church administrator, Shannon Turner, uploaded them to YouTube. I consider myself to be a pastor who utilizes his oratorical gifts to share the Good News via the spoken word more than through the written format. Even though I write sermons and other messages, I normally do so using an outline with various colors of ink. Placing my thoughts in a written manuscript is a challenge for me. However, with modern technology and the support and encouragement of my family, especially my wife Rosia and with the help of Joe Edd's wife, Sandi, I have been able to complete my first book.

It is my hope and desire to complete another book within the next 6-12 months that chronicles my journey as the first African American Senior pastor of the predominately white First United Methodist Church of Tupelo, MS from 2019-2022. I invite you to read it once it is published. My youngest daughter, Katelyn, wrote a poem when she was 9 years of age that is the impetus for this book

Martin Luther King, Jr. is his name

He didn't want a lot of fame.

Blacks and whites joining together; King thought this would take forever.

"I Have a Dream" was the name of his speech,

To make the world come to peace.

Martin Luther King helped pave the way.

Let's all join together and live his dream today.

Rev. Dr. Embra Jackson Jr.

Day 1

Prayer: Almighty and everlasting God, come touch us. Remind us that you are here always for us. Bless our time together that is devoted to you. In Thy name we pray, amen.

Scripture: Then, all the congregation raised a loud cry, and the people wept that night. And all the Israelites complained against Moses and Aaron; the whole congregation said to them, "Would that we had died in the land of Egypt! Or that we had died in this wilderness the Lord bringing us into this land to fall by the sword?" So, they said to one another, "let us choose a captain and go back to Egypt." Numbers 14:1-3

Reflection: What powerful words. The Israelites are complaining because things have become difficult, because even though they are no longer enslaved in Egypt, the unknown awaits them. Every now and then they grow hungry, they grow thirsty. So, they revolt against Moses and Aaron and ask why God placed them in this situation. Whenever we find ourselves in the wilderness, we often complain. We wonder why God has placed us in this situation. We want to return to Egypt, even to slavery, because it is the norm. Today, we are facing a great unknown. We don't know what the future holds. But we know Who holds the future.

When in uncertain times, if we are fortunate enough, we have A family. We have the church. We have our community. Most of all, we have God. Let us not complain as the children of Israel did. Rather let us have faith in an all-loving and an all-caring God. God does know our situation and God will be with us. God is holding our hands with His Mighty hand. God is assuring us that He who led the children out of Egypt will lead us through this wilderness of the Coronavirus. God never ever leave us or abandon us. We are children of God. And God loves us so much that he has promised always and everywhere to be with us. So have faith. Be firm in our convictions and know that God is with you. He is with me. God is with us all. We are not alone, even when we are in the wilderness. God, enable us to be touched by your Holy Spirit, so that we shall make it through this wilderness. We shall arrive at the promised land as the children of Israel did so many years ago.

Day 2

Prayer: God, we thank you for this day. And, even though we have challenges, we pray that you will continually be with us. In Thy name, amen.

Scripture: No, in all these things we are more than conquerors through Him who loved us. For I am convinced that neither death, nor life, nor angels, nor rulers, nor things present, nor things to come, nor powers, nor height, nor depth, nor anything else in all creation, will be able to separate us from the love of God in Christ Jesus our Lord. Romans 8: 37-39

Reflection: Living in quarantine and isolation produces loneliness and a sense of being separated from others as well as the body of Christ. During these times, we should be reminded of this scripture that tells us nothing will separate us from the love of Christ, not economic hardships, or war or even COVID. God is reminding us over and over that nothing—height, depth, not even death—will separate us from Christ. We need to continually look to the hills from whence cometh our help. Our help comes from the Lord who made heaven and earth. Let us remember that nothing separates us from the love of our Lord and Savior, Jesus Christ. May God bless you and be with you.

Day 3

Prayer: Almighty God, come now and touch us. Give us the strength and courage to withstand all of the pressures of life and the isolation and loneliness that have been presented to us. We pray for strength and courage. Amen.

Scripture: Now in Jerusalem by the Sheep Gate there is a pool called the Bethesda. It has five porticoes. In these lay many invalids — blind, lame, and paralyzed. One man was there who had been ill for 38 years. Jesus saw him lying there and knew he had been there a long time. Jesus said to him, "Do you want to be made well? The sick man answered him, "Sir, I have no one to put me into the pool when the water is stirred up; and while I am making my way, someone else steps down ahead of me." Jesus said to him," Stand up, take your mat, and walk." At once the man was made well, and he took up his mat and began to walk. John 5: 2-9a

Reflection: This scripture reminds us that Jesus is in the healing business. In spite of our infirmities, whether we are blind, lame, or paralyzed, or whatever our condition, Jesus is able to heal. This man had been ill for 38 long years. The first person in the pool was always healed. He had a long list of excuses why he could not get into the pool first when the angels came down and stirred it. In our lives, we have faced many trials and tribulations, especially during these times of great adversities. But I remind you, and myself — Jesus is still in the healing business. Through this time of being quarantined and separated from loved ones and fellow church members, Jesus promises us He will heal us of our infirmities. So, when Jesus asks, "Do you want to be healed?" Our answers should always be, "Yes, Lord, please heal me."

Day 4

Prayer: God be with us today. Strengthen us and give us the ability to always hold on to your steadfast hands. Help us find hope in your faithful presence. In Thy name, amen.

Scripture: Then Moses stretched out his hand over the sea. The Lord drove the sea back by a strong east wind all night and turned the sea into dry land; and the waters were divided. The Israelites went into the sea on dry ground, the waters forming a wall for them on their right and on their left. The Egyptians pursued, and went into the sea after them, all of Pharaoh's horses, chariots, and chariot drivers. At the morning watch the Lord in the pillar of fire and cloud looked down upon the Egyptian army and threw the Egyptian army into panic. He clogged their chariots wheels so that they turned with difficulty. The Egyptians said, "Let us flee from the Israelites, for the Lord is fighting for them against Egypt." Exodus 14:21-25

Reflection: This morning when I went outside, I saw several of my neighbors who are also church members. There was Michelle Hudson, John Morgan, in the rain. We greeted each other as normal, except that we had to remain more than six feet apart because of social distancing. For a preacher like me, that is very difficult. It brought to mind a movie, "The Ten Commandments," starring Charlton Heston, that I often watched when I was a child. It still comes on TV, and perhaps you have watched it. Today's scripture helps describe what happened in the movie and aids us in the midst of our crisis. Separation creates anxiety. Being confined to home and not being with one's loved ones or friends is very difficult during these times. But God reminds us that He will see us through the troubling waters and deliver us to the other side as he did the Israelites. Our message today is one of affirmation and assurance. Despite the walls of separation that now exist, God will see us from the side of anxiety and separation to the side of peace, to the side of love, to the side of a better tomorrow. We serve a God who is able. Today let us not fear but let us look to the Lord who is able to do not some things but all things

Day 5

Prayer: Almighty and everlasting God, come down, touch us, and fill us with your spirit. Remind us that we are not alone. Remind us, dear God, that this has been one of those seasons and that you will always be with us. In Christ's name, amen.

Scripture: For everything there is a season, and a time for every matter under heaven: a time to be born and a time to die; a time to plant, and a time to pluck up what is planted; a time to kill, and a time to heal; time to break down, and a time to build up; a time to weep, and a time to laugh; a time to mourn, and a time to dance; a time to throw away stones, and a time to gather stones together; a time to embrace, and a time to refrain from embracing; a time to seek, and a time to lose; a time to keep, and a time to throw away; a time to tear, and a time to sew; a time to keep silence, and a time to speak; a time to love, and a time to hate; a time for war, and the time for peace. Ecclesiastes 3:1-8.

Reflection: We are in a season of pain, suffering, isolation, and death. But today we need to be reminded that there is a better season. Job tells us that life is fleeting and full of trials and tribulations. But in the end, Job acknowledges that God is with us. The author of Ecclesiastes states the same theme. He says that in life we will have trials and tribulations, ups and downs, pains and sufferings. But in the end, the seasons of God never end. Because God is always with us. So, the word from God for us today is that this, too, shall pass. God is the author and finisher of all seasons. God has promised never ever to leave us alone. There is an old song that we used to sing that says we do not know what tomorrow shall bring. But we know Who holds tomorrow in his hand: our Lord and Savior Jesus Christ who was buried and rose from the dead. He is the mighty God. This season of darkness, pain, suffering, tears, and death will pass. We seek and cry out to you, Oh God. Remind us of a better season, that this too shall pass, and that you are always with us.

Day 6

Prayer: Dear God, come now. Remind us that you are already with us. Open our hearts and souls and minds to be receptive to your word today. In Christ, amen.

Scripture: When the righteous cry for help, the Lord hears and rescues them from all their troubles. The Lord is near to the brokenhearted and saves the crushed in spirit. Psalms 34:17-18

Reflection: In these short but powerful words, the Psalmist reminds us that troubles are part of life. But, what is fascinating, the Psalmist says that in spite of all of the trials and tribulations in this world, God will save us from all difficulties. Through natural disasters, financial crisis, illness, and even death, God has promised never ever to abandon us. This Psalm 34 must have really resonated with the Israelites because they had been through slavery, conquest, and many natural disasters. Through it all, they saw God working with them despite the difficulties that they faced. My word today is to let us be a people who, like the Psalmist, remembers that God hears and answers our prayers. God is with us, in spite of the circumstances that we face in this life. Hear again these words from the Psalmist, "when the righteous cry for help, the Lord hears and rescues them from all their troubles, the Lord is near to the brokenhearted and saves the crushed in spirit." Mighty God, we are brokenhearted. We feel crushed. Remind us that we are not alone, you are with us. You do hear prayer and you do answer prayer. Send your blessings down upon our church, upon our community, upon our nation, upon our world, upon us. And, even though we might feel crushed, remind us that you are a God who will uplift and save us. Amen.

Day 7

Prayer: Everlasting God, touch us. During this season of crisis and pandemic, restore wholeness and health to us. Remind us, you are still God.

Scripture: So he went down and immersed himself seven times in the Jordan, according to the word of the man of God ; his flesh was restored like the flesh of a young boy, and he was clean. (Kings II, 5:14)

Reflection: This is a story of Naaman, a great general of a foreign army, who had captured parts of Israel and taken away some of the people into captivity. One of these persons was a slave girl. Naaman, even though he was powerful, a great general and commander of the king's army, suffered from a disease we know as leprosy. Naaman sought healing. But no one could cure him. The unnamed slave girl told him if he returned to Israel, to seek the prophet Elijah, that Elijah could possibly heal him. He listened to her, sought Elijah, and found him. He expected Elijah to tell him, to be cured, to perform something great. Instead, Elijah told him to do something very simple. Go to the river Jordan and immerse himself seven times. Naaman refused. He was a great commander and wanted to do something great. Finally, he did as Elijah had requested. He went, washed himself seven times and a miracle occurred. He was healed.

    This story reminds me of our society today. We're looking for a cure for Covid 19. We want restoration from the Coronavirus. Scientists tell us that the best thing they can do at this time is to stay inside and away from gatherings and large crowds, to be isolated for a season. This simple request will slow down the spread of this deadly virus. Many of us think this is too simple. But, many times, God's word comes to us in simple ways. So today, I believe God is telling us that to be restored, we need to do that which is simple. My prayer today for you is to remain inside. to do the simple thing we have been asked to do to do. Through this simple thing, I believe God will bring healing and restoration.

Day 8

Prayer: Dear God, come now. Remind us again of the seasons of life. Watch over us during this time. Strengthen us and give us the ability always to trust and lean on you. Open our hearts, our souls, and our minds to be receptive to your word. In Your name, amen.

Scripture: This is what the Lord God showed me, a basket of summer fruit. He said, "Amos What do you see? And I said, "a basket of summer fruit." Amos 8:1-2

Reflection: This passage of scripture from Amos is very short. Some theologians will tell you that God is telling Amos to tell the people that the time is at an end. But when I read the passage of scripture about summer fruit, I thought about the seasons of life that were uplifted in a previous devotion. Rather than going outside, I looked around the house to see what decorations my wife might have reminding me that life is full of seasons. I found particular flowers that reminded me God provides for us in all circumstances and situations. I found a leaf, a reminder of the healing trees we have in the sanctuary at the church. During the season of Lent, and before worship services had been temporarily discontinued, we asked church members to gather leaves like these, place prayers on the back of them and hang them on real trees. David Shumaker, one of our associate pastors, had already uplifted this request on Facebook and the trees began to bud with leaves. This is a powerful reminder that God is able to bring life in all circumstances. Some of us feel as if we are barren. We have been abandoned and rejected. We feel all alone during times like this. But this passage of scripture from Amos, and the healing trees in our sanctuary, remind us that God is able to provide fruit, even in times like this. Remind us that even in the midst of winter, that you O God, provide for us. And, therefore, we do not worry or fear because you are God.

Day 9

Prayer: Dear God, come now. Remind us of your everlasting presence. Remind us that we are not alone, that you are with us. Bless and watch over us. Restore us. In Thy name, amen.

Scripture : "So I prophesied as I had been commanded; and as I prophesied, suddenly there was a noise, a rattling, and the bones came together, bone to its bone. I looked, and there were sinews on them, and flesh had come upon them, and skin had covered them; but there was no breath in them. Then he said to me, 'Prophesy to the breath, prophesy, mortal, and say to the breath: Thus says the Lord God: Come from the four winds, O breath, and breathe upon these slain, that they may live.' I prophesied as he commanded me, and the breath came into them, and they lived, and stood on their feet, a vast multitude." Ezekiel 37:7-10.

Reflection: This scripture, the story of the dry bones, is familiar to most of us. The dry bones represent Israel. The country has been conquered and taken away into captivity. The Israelites feel as if they are dead. The prophet, Ezekiel, comes and the Lord commands him to preach to these people, and remind them that they are not dead, that they shall live again. The analogy of the dry bones represents us today, and humanity in general. Whenever we face trials and tribulations in this life, many times we feel as though we are defeated. We want to give up, we are dismayed, we feel isolated and separated. We feel like all life is lost. But Ezekiel is reminding us today, as God reminded him to preach to the people of Israel, that if they put their faith, hope, and trust in almighty God, who is able to do all things, that even dry bones can live again. So today, in spite of what you might be going through in your life, whether it's difficulties at home with your spouse or children, or job difficulties at work, during battles with this Covid pandemic, God wants us to remember that He is able to do everything. Our prayer today is that we do not lose faith and hope but remain firm, knowing that even dry bones can live again, because we serve a God who is able to do all things.

_____

_____

_____

_____

_____

_____

_____

Day 10

Prayer: Almighty and everlasting God, come touch us with your Holy healing spirit. Instead of the calamities of life, we ask for Your peace, the peace you have promised always and everywhere to be with us. Strengthen and guide us. In Your name, amen.

Scripture: But soon a violent wind, called the northeaster, rushed down from Crete. We were scarcely able to get the boat under control. We were being pounded by the storm so violently that on the next day they began to throw the cargo overboard. When neither sun nor stars appeared for many days all hope of being saved was at last abandoned. Paul then stood up among them and said, "I urge you now to keep up your courage ... do not be afraid ... for I have faith in God .... Acts 27:13-25

Reflection: This passage of scripture reminds us that Paul was headed to Rome to be imprisoned. He was on a ship and a great storm arose. And the sailors became frightened. But Paul, like Jesus, when the storm arose on the Sea of Galilee, remained calm. And like Jesus, Paul was able to remain calm because he had faith and in an all loving and all-powerful God. Calamities, storms, trials, and tribulations come to us in our lives. But like Paul, and like Jesus, we are reminded to keep our eyes on the distant shore. Because we know that God is able to calm the stormy seas of life. And so, during this time, if you are having difficulty at home, school, work, church, your business, whatever calamities the pandemic has brought upon you, keep our eyes on the distant shore, keep our eyes on Jesus Christ. Jesus can calm even the stormy seas. Have faith that God is able to bring calmness in this storm. God will see us through this storm. Many are fearful and don't know where to turn or what to do. But keep your faith. God is constantly with us.

Day 11

Prayer: Almighty and everlasting, all powerful God, come now. Calm your people. Give us the assurance to know that we are not abandoned. That we are not alone. That you are our refuge and our strength, our very present help in times of trouble. Be with us during this time of pandemic, dear God. Allow us to remain firm holding on to your unchanging hands. In Jesus Christ. Amen.

Scripture: God is our refuge and strength, a very present help in trouble. Therefore, we will not fear though the earth should change, though the mountains shake in the heart of the sea, though its waters roar and foam, though the mountains tremble with its tumult "Be still and know that I am God! I am exalted among the nations and exalted in the earth." The Lord of hosts is with us; the God of Jacob is our refuge. Psalm 46: 4-7; 10-11

Reflection: During times like these, many of us ask questions: "Why is this happening?" "Where can I turn for help?" We turn to the government and there seems to be limited answers. We ask friends and neighbors. Many times, they are unable to help us. We turn to the church and the church is not able to help. But I am convinced, we have a God who is able to provide an answer. The Book of Psalms in general and Psalm 46 in particular affirm that God is always with us. The Psalms reflect on life being full of problems. Life is full of trials and tribulations. Life is full of storms, such as the ones we are currently facing regarding the pandemic for Coronavirus. But in the midst of the roaring seas, in the midst of the storm, in the midst of earthquakes, in the midst of all of the trials and tribulations of life, God, through it all is still God, even though we might be anxious, upset, perhaps even fearful, God is still God. He will never, ever leave us alone. So let us take heart and not fear, but instead rely on God. Because we know that our help comes from the Lord who made heaven and earth. That is power. Amen!

Day 12

Prayer: Almighty and everlasting God, come touch us. We remember that through it all we are not alone. God, we trust and depend upon your word. Reach out and touch those who are hearing these words this day. And let us know that you, God, are still there for us and are with us. And that somehow, you will be with us through it all and that we can trust and depend on your word. In thy name we pray, amen.

Reflection: I wish that I had a great voice for singing. But unfortunately, I do not. I love good music. I love rhythm. I love the words of songs. Today's devotion is one of my favorite songs from Andre Crouch. I'd like to share some of these words with you. And again, if I could sing I would. But these words I think are very powerful. Even without Covid 19, life can be difficult. The words to this song were written before the Coronavirus pandemic was part of our lives. However, Andre Crouch, the writer of this song, went through some difficult times in his life. In the words of this song, he is telling us that through it all, God has promised to be with us. *"Through it all, through it all, I've learned to trust in Jesus. I've learned to trust in God. Through it all through it all I've learned to depend upon His Word."* And that is my word for us today. Through it all. Learn how to depend and trust on God's Word.

I've had many tears and sorrows
I've had questions for tomorrow
There's been times I didn't
know right from wrong
But in every situation
God gave me blessed consultation
That my trials come only to make me strong
I've been to a lot of places
And I've seen a million faces
But in my lonely hours
Yes, those precious lonely hours
Jesus let me know that I was his own
That's the reason I say that
Through it all
Through it all

I've learned to trust in Jesus
I've learned to trust in God
I've learned to depend upon his word
So, I thank God for the mountains
And I thank him for the valleys
And I thank him for the storms
he brought me through
For I've never had a problem
I've never known that God could solve them
I've never known what faith in his word could do
That's the reason I say
Through it all
Through it all
I've learned to depend upon his word
Though it all.

Song *Through It All* by Andre Crouch

Day 13

Prayer: Almighty God, open our hearts and souls and minds to be receptive to your word today. Remove fear from our hearts and allow us to acknowledge that you, God, are always with us. In your name we pray. Amen.

Scripture: Our Father, who art in heaven, hallowed be thy name, thy kingdom come, thy will be done on earth as it is in heaven. Give us this day our daily bread and forgive us our trespasses as we forgive those who trespass against us. And lead us not into temptation, but deliver us from evil, for thine is the kingdom and the power and the glory forever. Amen. Matthew 6:9-13; Luke 11:2-4

Reflection: At First United Methodist Church, Tupelo, Mississippi, we are preaching a sermon series entitled "Deliver us from Evil." As part of that sermon series, we are encouraging our members to read a very small but powerful book by Wesley Hill, *The Lord's Prayer*. In this book, Wesley Hill expounds on each section of *The Lord's Prayer*. A portion of what he conveys is that we Christians believe that we have already, in part, been delivered from evil, because Jesus came and defeated the devil. But the fulfillment of the kingdom of God, at this point in history, is not totally at hand. In his book Wesley emphasizes that God has promised always to be with us. Wesley also explores how the disciples came to Jesus and said, Lord, teach us how to pray. And Jesus taught them what we know today as "The Lord's Prayer."

The brief yet powerful words of this prayer remind us that we are not alone, that God has overcome all evil. Therefore, we, as a Christian people of faith, are called to trust and depend upon God, and be reminded that we have a God who is able to defeat all evil. We reaffirm our commitment and faith in an all-loving and all-powerful God. Even though the news may seem to be more than we can bear, the sickness from the Coronavirus and the evil in the world often seem to overwhelm us. Through The Lord's Prayer, we are taught that God will deliver us from evil. God will deliver us from this virus. He will deliver us from war and pestilence. He will deliver us from all that harms and impacts us in a negative way. God, constantly help us to recall that we are people who have been called by You to be faithful and remain faithful to You, knowing that everything will be okay because You are God. Remind us that we truly have been delivered from evil.

Day 14

Prayer: We ask you, God, to be with us today, strengthening us during this time of darkness as we continually look for the light. In Your Name, amen.

Scripture: On that day, when evening had come, he said to them, "Let us go across to the other side." And leaving the crowd behind, they took him with them in the boat, just as he was. Other boats were with him. A great windstorm arose, and the waves beat into the boat, so that the boat was already being swamped. But he was in the stern asleep on the cushion; and they woke him up and said to him, "Teacher, do you not care that we are perishing?" He woke up and rebuked the wind, and said to the sea, "Peace! Be still!" Then the winds ceased, and there was a dead calm. He said to them, "Why are you afraid? Have you still no faith?" And they were filled with great awe and said to one another, "Who then is this, that even the wind and the sea obey him?" Mark 4:35-41

Reflection: Life is different in today's world. We still need our medical personnel to advise us. But we also need the great physician, Jesus Christ. In this scripture, faith and fear are the focus. Jesus is in the boat with his disciples. A great storm arises. The disciples react with fear, as we normally do in similar situations. Jesus calmed the sea and reminded them that fear, and faith seldom coexist. He reminded them that they are supposed to be people of faith, that God will never ever abandon them. In this scripture, today Jesus reminds us that even when the storms of life are raging, He is with us.

Day 15

Prayer: Oh God, come now and hear our prayers. Look down from heaven upon us, upon those who are suffering the loss of loved ones, those who have lost a job and are anxious and nervous. Send your blessings upon us. And remind us also God, that this, too, shall pass and that we are your children. In thy name, amen.

Scripture: When they say, "There is peace and security," then sudden destruction will come upon them, as labor pains come upon a pregnant woman, and there will be no escape ... For God has destined us not for wrath but for obtaining salvation through our Lord Jesus Christ, who died for us, so that whether we are awake or asleep we might live with him. I Thessalonians 5:3; 9-10.

Reflection: These words of Scripture are very powerful for those who are going through trials and tribulations. Paul compares life to a woman who is delivering a child while going through labor pains. That life is full of travails, but God does not want us to always suffer. God will save us. And as a mother has her newborn child, the joy of seeing that new infant, many times helps the pain of the delivery to subside. So, it is with the troubles of life. We suffer for a while, but one day God will save us.

Today, we are in similar labor pains. We are hurting. We are suffering. We are isolated. We are distanced one from another. Life seems, as I explained to someone the other day, like we are living in a nightmare. And I want to pinch myself to wake up. This is a reality of our current situation. But I am reminded that our Lord Jesus Christ, who died for us according to the words here in scripture, has promised us that God will save us and that we are God's people. Today the message is one of hope of a better future. And more than that, a message of salvation. God will never ever abandon us or leave us all by ourselves. God will save us. Let us remember these words. Let us remember that we are not alone. God will be with us. God is for us, and we will be saved because we are God's children.

_____

_____

_____

_____

_____

_____

_____

Day 16

Prayer: Almighty God come now and give us clean hearts, restore our spirits, and protect us during this time of pandemic. Reaffirm for us of your continued presence and that we are not alone. You have promised always and, in all circumstances, to be with us, even during a pandemic.

Scripture: Create in me a clean heart, O God, and put a new and right spirit within me. Do not cast me away from your presence, and do not take your holy spirit from me. Restore to me the joy of your salvation and sustain in me a willing spirit. Psalm 51:10-12

Reflection: During this season of crisis in which we find ourselves, we often want help. During these times, we need to turn to God's word. The Book of Psalms is full of inspiration and distressful words. But more than anything else, Psalms is a book full of hope, of restoration. The scripture reading today reminds us, as usual, that we are not alone. That it is okay to cry. It is okay to question why this is happening. It is okay to even be upset. We are also reminded that when we pray to God and ask God to be with us, God has promised us His Presence.

As Christians, when we read scripture and we pray, we are a people who know that God will never ever abandon us or leave us alone. Even though we read scripture and pray, sometimes we cry to God because of our circumstances. Today, some of us are crying to God because of our circumstances. The Psalmist reminds us that God, because He loves us, can and will always be with us. God loves us so much that He sent His only begotten Son Jesus into the world. And because of that Divine action, I am convinced that this time shall pass, and that God will sustain us and be with us. My word to us today is to not lose faith or hope. We should Remember that we are people who are loved by God and that God is able to look beyond all of our faults and to see our needs and always be with us.

Day 17

Prayer. Almighty and everlasting God, touch our hearts, our souls, our minds to be receptive to your guidance this day and forever. In Thy name we pray, amen.

Scripture: And I tell you, you are Peter, on this rock I will build my church, and the gates of Hades will not prevail against it. Matthew 16:18

Reflection: Recently, when I was in the office, I looked at our pictorial directory. The caption beneath the picture on the cover of the directory includes the scripture referenced above (Matthew, the 16th chapter, verse 18: *"Upon this rock, I will build my church."*) In the directory are pictures of the members and various activities in the church. Also, on the cover is a collage, like a puzzle, composed of pictures of the members. That collage, and the words of scripture from Matthew, remind us of what Jesus told Peter, that upon this rock, I will build this church, and the gates of hell shall not prevail against it.

For those of you who are members of First United Methodist Church, Tupelo, this directory is a reminder of who we are and whose we are. Our church is not just a religious institution, but a group of people of faith is built upon the rock known as Jesus Christ. Nothing shall prevail against the church, or God's people. We are people who have a firm foundation. Our foundation is not built upon sand, but rather is built upon the solid foundation of Jesus Christ. "On Christ, the solid rock I stand, all other ground is sinking sand." Let us remember that during these times of pandemic, these times of job loss and of anxiety, that our faith is built upon the solid rock that is God. When we feel like we are losing our way or feel like we have been abandoned and have nowhere to turn, remind us, oh God, that you are the solid rock upon which our faith is built.

_____
_____
_____
_____
_____
_____
_____

Day 18

Prayer: God, we thank you for this day. We thank you for your blessings. Hold our hand, dear God, and do not let us stumble and fall headlong. Instead, lead us by thy righteous mighty hand. In the name of Jesus Christ, amen.

Scripture: Our steps are made firm by the Lord, when he delights in our way; though we stumble, we shall not fall headlong, for the Lord holds us by the hand. Psalm 37:23-24

Reflection: During this time of pandemic, there seems to be a lot of stumbling going on. Nations are competing against nations for masks and various medical equipment. Scientists are racing for solutions to the Covid virus. States are competing with one another for respirators. Cities and county governments and state governments seem confused about what to do or where to turn. We seem to be stumbling all over ourselves. When I look at the news, I am amazed and dismayed at what I see. I look for a solution, but none seems to be forthcoming.

However, when I read today's scripture, Psalm 37, I know that God says, "though we stumble, we shall not fall headlong. For the Lord holds us by the hand." This passage is an analogy for me of one of my grandchildren when she was learning to walk. It took her a little longer than the others to walk. We would hold her hand as she learned to walk. If we let her hand go, and she realized that we were not holding on, she would stumble and tumble over. Finally, she learned how to walk, but it took some time. And it took us constantly holding her hand and reassuring her. God, like a parent, is holding our hands during this time. God, like a parent or grandparent, is encouraging us. God, like a parent or grandparent, is reminding us that we are not alone. God is reminding us that we shall stumble from time to time, but we shall not fall headlong into the abyss.

Day 19

Prayer: God, come and touch us, fill us with your spirit. Even though we know that life is full of trials and tribulations, in the midst of it all you have promised always, in every way, to be with us, to strengthen and guide us. In Your name we pray. Amen.

Scripture: Then Jesus went with them to a place called Gethsemane; and he said to his disciples, "Sit here while I go over there and pray." He took with him Peter and the two sons of Zebedee and began to be grieved and agitated. Then he said to them, "I am deeply grieved, even unto death; remain here, and stay awake with me." And going a little farther, he threw himself on the ground and prayed, "My Father, if it is possible, let this cup pass from me.; yet not what I want but what you want." Matthew 26:36-39

Reflection: Today's devotion is being recorded in our chapel at the church. This lovely building was built when Reverend Dr. Prentiss Gordon was the pastor. It was created for small weddings, baptisms, funerals, etc. Today, it is a reminder when Jesus gathered with his disciples in the garden of Gethsemane. The Scripture for today tells us that even Jesus suffered and was challenged by death. He knew he would soon be betrayed. He was spit upon. A crown of thorns placed upon his head. He knew that he would be pierced on the side. When he cried out on the cross, vinegar, rather than water, was given to him. He knew that he would die between two criminals. Also, the scripture conveys that Jesus cried out, "Father, my Father, let this cup pass from my lips." But then he ends by saying, "Not my will be done, but yours."

Often in life, our will appears to be the opposite of God's will. Often, our minds do not distinguish or understand and accept, that God's will is always supreme. That he is with us, even amid our suffering. And even though Jesus knew he was suffering, he knew he would not be totally abandoned by God. God the Father would always be with him. Even though Jesus cried out, "Let this cup pass from me," he ended that prayer by saying, "Not My, but Thy will be done." Today, amid all the trials and tribulations we are facing, some of us may be crying out to God, "Let this cup pass from our lives." But we know that it is not our will, but God's will that prevails. God will be with us as He was with Jesus. We may suffer, and our weeping may endure for a night. But joy comes in the morning. Our powerful God is with us during our time of suffering.

Day 20

Prayer: Lord, please be with us today as we prepare to share what you have given to me to share with your people.

Scripture: While they were eating, Jesus took a loaf of bread, and after blessing it he broke it, gave it to his disciples and said, "Take, eat; this is my body." Then he took a cup, and after giving thanks he gave it to them, saying, "Drink from it, all of you; for this is my blood of the covenant, which is poured out for many for the forgiveness of sins. I tell you; I will never again drink of this fruit of the vine until that day when I drink it new with you in my Father's kingdom." Matthew 26:26-29

Reflection: This scripture reminds us how Jesus, while in the upper room, commemorated the Passover Meal by instituting a new one. We now call it Holy Communion or The Lord's Supper. One of the things that grieves us greatly at this church during his time of epidemic is being unable to have holy communion in person. But this scripture tells us that Jesus Christ knows our hearts, our souls, and our minds. And we can still be connected one with another even if we are not physically in the same room. But most of all, we can be connected with God in spite of the physical space.

When Jesus instituted The Lord's Supper, He said, "Drink from this, all of you. This is my blood of the covenant, which is poured out for you for the forgiveness of sins." Through this sacrament, Jesus is telling us that we are connected, that we are one body, we are one loaf. Even though physically we are all separated, God is still with us. And we are still one in the Spirit. So, we grieve that we cannot meet together face to face and break the bread and pass the cup. But in spirit, I break the bread and give it to you this day. In His Spirit, I give you the cup of salvation. In His Spirit, we are connected. And You, O God, are present with us.

Day 21

Prayer: Almighty and everlasting God, come, touch us, heal us. Allow us to be open and receptive to your guidance. Protect us during this time. In thy name, amen.

Scripture: "Have I not commanded you, be strong and be of good courage. Do not be frightened, and neither be dismayed. For the Lord your God is with you, wherever you go." Joshua 1:9

Reflection: What powerful words. Remember the story of Moses and the children of Israel being released from bondage in Egypt and going into the promised land. As they entered the Promised Land, they met people they thought were giants. Joshua eventually led the people into the promised land with a realization that God had promised them this land, and that God would never ever abandon or leave them. Listen to these words again, and hopefully you will find courage within them. "Have I not commanded you, be strong, and be of good courage? Do not be frightened, neither be dismayed. For the Lord, your God is with you, wherever you go."

During these times of pandemic, times of uncertainty, times of fear, times of isolation and separation, times of death, we are reminded that there was a Good Friday. But there also was an Easter Sunday morning. We are reminded that God promises us that we are not alone and that we should be strong, we should be courageous. Even when facing what seems like overwhelming odds, God is still with us, sitting high on the throne.

So, whenever we are fearful. Whenever we are nervous. Whenever life seems to be overwhelming you with all the reports regarding what is going on in the world. Remember these words; 'be strong and be of good courage. Be not frightened, be not dismayed. For the Lord, your God is with you wherever you go.' Let us not be frightened. Let us not be nervous. Let us put all of our faith and hope and trust in God.

Day 22

Prayer: Almighty and everlasting God, come fill us with your Holy Spirit. Give us the perseverance we need to run this race that we call life. Give us strength, courage, and faith. This we ask in thy name. Amen.

Scripture: Therefore, since we are surrounded by so great a cloud of witnesses, let us also lay aside every weight and the sin that clings so closely, and let us run with perseverance the race that is set before us, looking to Jesus the pioneer and perfecter of our faith, who for the sake of the joy that was set before him endured the cross, disregarding its shame, and has taken his seat at the right hand of the throne of God. Hebrews 12:1-2

Reflection: Recently, I was preparing a funeral message of one of our long-standing members. And the family suggested that this passage is one of the texts that could be used for the service. I was not able to attend the funeral because I was being quarantined for 14 days with my family. But I had written a message for the family. Generally, the message was this: Your loved one has run the race. He has finished his course. And now is set for him in heaven, a heavenly crown.

As I thought about the life of this person who was now deceased, I also thought about the Coronavirus and the crisis and the pandemic that we are facing. It is a race that is set before us. But God, through these words, tell us that we need to lay aside the weights that are holding us down—the weights of fear, the weights of shame, the weights of anxiety, the weights of depression, the weights that bear us down because of not knowing what tomorrow will bring. But God and these scriptures are a challenge for us to continue to run the race called life. If we lay aside some of these weights, it makes the running easier. It is not easy to lay aside fear and anxiety when every morning we read about the number of persons who have tested positive for the virus, about the number of persons who have died. But I believe that God wants us to continue to run the race. God wants us to lay aside these weights until we reach the finish line. God will be with us, and we will be victorious. We shall overcome these challenges because we are running the race, not for ourselves, but for our loved ones. And God will be there at the finish line.

Day 23

Prayer: God, come and protect us. Guide us during this time of crisis and pandemic. Come God and give us strength and courage to hold on to your unchanging hands. This we ask through your Son, Jesus Christ, and through Thy Holy Spirit, amen.

Scripture: You who live in the shelter of the Most High, who abide in the shadow of the Almighty, will say to the Lord, "My refuge and my fortress, my God, in whom I trust." For he will deliver you from the snare of the fowler and from the deadly pestilence; he will cover you with his pinions, and under his wings you will find refuge; his faithfulness is a shield and a buckler. You will not fear the terror of the night, or the arrow that flies by day, or the pestilence that stalks in darkness, or the destruction that wastes at noonday ... For he will command his angels concerning you to guard you in all your ways. On their hands they will bear you up, so that you will not dash your foot against a stone. Psalm 91:1-6; 11-12

Reflection: It is easy to become discouraged, frightened, depressed during times like these—reading the paper, turning on the television, looking at news. We seem to hear nothing but bad news. Many become frightened and fearful of what the future might hold. But the Psalmist states that we are not alone. We are not alone; God will be there when we need Him. God will send His angels to protect us and to guide us even when all seems hopeless and helpless, even when we feel trapped by despair. These brief, yet powerful, words confirm that God is our help in times of trouble. Sometimes at night, I become depressed after hearing projections in the news that tell how many people have been exposed to the virus and how many might die. But then I read these words, "For God will command his angels concerning us to guard us in all ways. And on their hands, they will bear us up so that we will not dash our foot against a stone." What powerful words are these? God will send His angels to guide and protect us. Whenever you are despondent or fearful, please remember God's angels are here for us.

Day 24

Prayer: Dear God, open our hearts and minds to your word today. May we feel your presence in and through them. In Your name, amen

Scripture: "But Mary stood weeping outside the tomb. As she wept, she bent over to look into the tomb; and she saw two angels in white, sitting where the body of Jesus had been lying, one at the head and the other at the feet. They said to her, "Woman, why are you weeping?" She said to them, "They have taken away my Lord, and I do not know where they have laid him." When she had said this, she turned around and saw Jesus standing there, but she did not know that it was Jesus. Jesus said to her, "Woman, why are you weeping? Whom are you looking for?" Supposing him to be the gardener, she said to him, "Sir, if you have carried him away, tell me where you have laid him, and I will take him away." Jesus said to her, "Mary!" She turned and said to him in Hebrew, "Rabbouni!" (Which means Teacher). Jesus said to her, "Do not hold on to me, because I have not yet ascended to the Father. But go to my brothers and say to them, 'I am ascending to my Father and your father, to my God and your God.'" Mary Magdalene went and announced to the disciples, "I have seen the Lord;" and she told them that he had said these things to her. John 20:11-18

Reflection: Easter morning. The time of year when the church gathers, we usually wear out festive colors. The church is full of people. (Some, perhaps, that we have not seen for quite some time.) This is a day of joy, a day of celebration, Easter egg hunts, flowers, Easter lilies, remembering all that the resurrection brings. These powerful words from John's Gospel convey for us that Mary was weeping because Jesus had been crucified and buried in a borrowed tomb. The angels appear to her and ask her the question, why are you weeping? Jesus appears to her, but she does not recognize him, and he asked her the same question. "Why are you weeping?"

Today, I ask us the same question on this Easter Sunday morning of 2020. Why are we weeping? Perhaps some of you are saying we are weeping because we've lost loved ones. We are weeping because we are fearful. We are weeping because we don't know what tomorrow will hold.

But these words from God, and from John, remind us that Christianity is based upon the solid foundation of the resurrection. Jesus rose on the third day, with all power in his hand. We have no fear in our hearts, because the day is Easter Sunday. My Word to us today is let us not be fearful. Let us be a people of faith. Because the story is told over and over and over again, that Jesus died on the cross. But on the third day, he rose with all power in his hands. We are people whom Jesus loves. Therefore, let us celebrate this Easter Sunday with joy, even amidst the sorrow and pain.

Day 25

Prayer: May God continue to bless and watch over each and every one of you and provide comfort through this devotion.

Scripture: Now Jesus did many other signs in the presence of his disciples, which are not written in this book. But these are written so that you may come to believe that Jesus is the Messiah, the Son of God, and that through believing you may have life in his name. John 20:30-31

Reflection: Easter Sunday is generally a high day in the life of our church. The Sunday after Easter is low in attendance. People seem not to be as excited as usual. But this devotion's scripture will help us as we transition from the Easter celebration to the post Easter time in the life of the church. Prior to writing these words, the author of the Gospel of John tells the story of Jesus' death on the cross and his burial in a tomb. And then on Easter, the story of his resurrection. He concludes this Gospel with the reason he has written these words. John says, "I wrote these stories about Jesus because I want all who read these words to believe that Jesus is the Son of God, the Messiah, the long awaited Anointed One. And through believing in Him, you might be saved."

Today, we need to hear these words more than ever. Life is much different today than ever before. We have celebrated Easter, but perhaps there are those who still are sad. Perhaps there are those who are still anxious and worried. But John tells us why he wrote these words about Jesus and the disciples and the miracles that Jesus performed. He wants us to be reminded that there was a resurrection on Easter Sunday morning. And because of that event, Jesus lives. We also can live and have everlasting life. So, let us not lose hope. Let us not lose faith. Let us not become despondent. Rather let us celebrate as people of hope and faith, knowing that through God, all things are possible.

_____

_____

_____

_____

_____

_____

_____

Day 26

Prayer: God, come and touch us, fill us with your Holy Spirit. Remind us that even though Easter has passed, you are still with us and will never, ever abandon us. Open our hearts and minds and souls to be receptive to your word today. In Thy name, amen.

Scripture: Now the eleven disciples went to Galilee, to the mountain to which Jesus had directed them. When they saw him, they worshipped him; but some doubted. And Jesus came and said to them, "All authority in heaven and on earth has been given to me. Go therefore and make disciples of all nations, baptizing them in the name of the Father and of the Son and of the Holy Spirit, and teaching them to obey everything that I have commanded you. And remember, I am with you always, to the end of the age." Mathew 28:16-20

Reflection: These last words of Jesus, written by the gospel writer of Matthew, are called the commissioning of the disciples. This is known as The Great Commission. It reminds us of what Jesus has called us to do. Even in a time of pandemic, Jesus still wants us to reach out and tell others about the glory, the magnificence, and the love of Jesus Christ. Jesus tells the disciples that even though he will no longer physically be with them, he says, "I am with you always, to the end of the age."

Today, these words are more powerful than perhaps at any other time in human history. We need to hear them and be reminded that Jesus told the disciples these words prior to ascending into heaven. As we hear them again, may they give us comfort and remember, "I am with you always, to the end of the age." God is still with us. Jesus promised to always be with us. Today, whenever we feel like we are alone, whenever we feel like we cannot move forward, recall the words of Jesus Christ to the disciples at the end of the Gospel of Matthew, "I am with you always to the end of the age." Let us find comfort. Let us find peace. Let us find security in the words of our Lord and Savior Jesus Christ. God come and fulfill your promise to be with us. Let us find comfort and peace in these words. Amen.

Day 27

Prayer: God, touch these Thy people. Touch all of us, and allow us to be at peace, to rejoice in you, and to know, dear God, that this too shall pass because you are God. In the name of Jesus Christ, the resurrected Lord, amen.

Scripture: Rejoice in the Lord always; again, I will say, Rejoice. Let your gentleness be known to everyone. The Lord is near. Do not worry about anything, but in everything by prayer and supplication with thanksgiving let your requests be known to God. And the peace of God, which passes all understanding, will guard your hearts and your minds in Christ Jesus. Philippians 4:4

Reflection: As usual, the scriptures have very, very powerful words for us today. Paul, in his letter to the church at Philippi, reminds them that they should rejoice always. In every circumstance, they should always give praise to God. In spite of how dark or gloomy life may seem, they should constantly rely on God, because God will give them, regardless of the circumstances in which they find themselves, the peace that passes all human understanding,

In the midst of this pandemic, Paul's message is emphasizing that even in the midst of the trials and tribulations of life, God has promised always to be with us. And as a result, we can rejoice. This rejoicing is not a "ha ha" happiness that is not facing the current reality. But rather, it is that peace that Paul talks about, to be at peace even in the midst of trials and tribulations. So, God's word for us today is this: Rejoice in the Lord always. And again, I say rejoice. And the peace of God, which passes all understanding, will guard our hearts and our minds in Christ Jesus.

Day 28

Prayer: God, come and touch us with your Holy Spirit. Make us realize, Dear God, that you are with us and that we are not alone. We ask this most humbly in the name of the Father, Son, and through the Holy Spirit, amen.

Scripture: "Humble yourselves therefore under the mighty hand of God, so that he may exalt you in due time. Cast all your anxiety on him because he cares for you. Discipline yourselves, keep alert. Like a roaring lion your adversary the devil prowls around, looking for someone to devour. Resist him, steadfast in your faith, for you know that your brothers and sisters in all the world are undergoing the same kinds of suffering. And after you have suffered for a little while, the God of all grace, who has called you to his eternal glory in Christ, will himself restore, support, strengthen, and establish you. To him be the power forever and ever. Amen." 1 Peter 5:6-11

Reflection: Peter reminds us that God is saying that life is full of adversities. Those who would bring us harm are often led to do so because of evil intent. But, also, life is full of challenges, such as illness, divorce, alcohol and drug addiction, war, the pandemic that we're facing. Peter says that we ought to resist evil and rely on God for our salvation. We should humble ourselves and look to God who will, in due course, vindicate us and uplift us. Because of the overwhelming adversities that we face in life, it may not seem that God is on our side. But this passage of scripture says that we are to humble ourselves and look to God for guidance, direction, and protection. And that God will restore us, support us, strengthen, and establish us. These are the words of God that hopefully will give us the strength and courage to hold on to God's unchanging hands. God will never ever fail to fulfill his promises. God come down is our world today. These words from First Peter affirm that God is in the midst of the trials and tribulations of life. God is in the midst of this pandemic.

Day 29

Prayer: God, come and touch us. Fill us with your Holy Spirit. Open our hearts, souls, and minds to be receptive to your word. We ask that you would be with us during this time of trial and tribulation. May I be able to be used by you to say something to help somebody along this journey of life. This most humbly in Your name, amen.

Scripture: In my distress I called upon the Lord; to my God I cried for help. From his temple he heard my voice, and my cry to him reached his ears. Psalm 18:6

Reflection: During these times of pandemic, these times of stress, isolation, separation, and depression that many of us may be experiencing, we often cry tears of sadness and tears of anxiety. The Psalmist tells us that God hears our cries and responds. As a child, I remember getting in trouble and perhaps getting a spanking or some other form of punishment. I remember trying to cry as loud as I could so that my father or mother would soon release from their spanking or the punishment that I was experiencing. Sometimes it worked. I recall these times when I read this passage of scripture. Whenever we are hurting, and whenever we are in pain, we want someone to hear us and to understand and to comprehend our pain and our suffering. God is still sitting high on the throne and God is able to hear our cry. The Psalmist says from his temple, the Lord heard his voice, his cry came to God's ears.

Whenever we are stressed, whenever we seem overwhelmed, whenever life seems more than we can bear, remember these words. God is able to hear our cries and will respond to us. So today, in case you are experiencing pain and suffering, in case you do not know where to turn or what to do, it's okay to cry, to cry out until the Lord hears and responds to our cries and our pleas. Oh, God, we cry out to you today to hear our cries and to be with us and never abandon us. Remind us dear God, that you are able to wipe the tears from our eyes and that we are not alone.

Day 30

Prayer: God, allow us to be able to receive your blessings. We ask and pray that you will continue to watch over us. In Thy name, amen.

Scripture: And God is able to provide you with every blessing in abundance, so that by always having enough of everything, you may share abundantly in every good work. 2 Corinthians 9:8

Reflection: God is conveying to us through this passage of scripture that God is able to bless us abundantly. And not just sometimes, but Paul says at all times, and in all things. God will take care of our needs. And we will abound in God's gracious creation, and gifts of abundance in our lives. Sometimes it does not feel as if God is blessing us or that we are receiving God's boundless gifts. But as we reflect upon our lives, even when challenges come, we have been blessed by God with life itself. Many of us have been blessed with loving families. We have been blessed with church members and pastors who love and care for us. We have been blessed to live in a country that is a blessing. We are truly blessed even during times like this pandemic.

In our suffering, God will continue to bless us. In the midst of our strain, even in the midst of our pandemic, even when all seems to be going wrong in the world. God is reminding us that he will never ever forget about us, that we are not alone. God will truly continue to bless and watch over us. And so, whatever you are experiencing in your life today, in spite of the pain and suffering that you may be going through, God wants you to know that He will continually bless us and watch over us. We are blessed by God and one day, this too, shall pass.

Day 31

Prayer: God, come now, touch us, and guide us. Teach us to be patient, teach us to wait on you and remind us in waiting, that you will take care of us. In Thy name, amen.

Scripture: My soul waits for the Lord more than those who watch for the morning. Psalm 130:6

Reflection: I was recently in a line at a store. I don't remember the exact details, but I do remember the feeling of being impatient. The line was moving slowly. I wanted to move ahead quickly because I needed to get home and take care of some business. I grew more and more impatient. Finally, the line moved, and I was able to receive the service that I was seeking. But it brought to memory that in life, we often have to wait. Many times, we have to wait to receive blessings. And every now and then we have to wait on the Lord. The Lord's time is not our time.

During this time of pandemic, there is a debate about when we ought to come out of quarantine, when the self-isolation will end, when the stay-at-home ought to be over. Many people are pushing for a quick time for us to be relieved from the stress of being at home and being locked away from loved ones. The Psalmist's words in this devotional's scripture, remind us that a watchman would keep watch over the city all night, from a walled area to look for enemies that might be approaching, or look for danger of any kind. And if danger approached, he would blow a horn to let people know that danger was coming. In the midst of his duty, he had to stay awake. Unlike the disciples who were with Jesus in the Garden of Gethsemane, who went to sleep on more than one occasion, and were rebuked by Jesus. The watchman had to stay awake all night and had to be patient. God is telling us today that we have to be patient. God is reminding us through this psalm that we have to be patient, that often our time is not the same as God's time. This is not a message that is easy to hear. We want to have things immediately. We have instant food, microwave, instant TV, everything has to happen all of a sudden. But every now and then, God tells us to slow down, to calm down, to be at peace, to relax and to know that I am God. And I will take care of this. So those of us today who are anxious or burdened with waiting, just relax. Remember that God holds the whole wide world in his hands. And that God's time is God's time and that everything will be okay. Because God is still God.

Day 32

Prayer: Now I lay me down to sleep, I pray the Lord my soul to keep, If I should die before I wake, I pray the Lord my soul to take.

Scripture: I lie down and sleep; I wake again, for the Lord sustains me. Psalm 3:5

Reflection: How many of you remember, as a child, saying our evening prayer? I used to say that prayer every night as a child and found comfort in it. It was simple, it was easy to remember. And something about the words gave me comfort. Even though looking back now as a pastor, and as an adult, those little words can be disturbing because they talk about perhaps dying in the night. I am reminded when I repeat those words, I lie down and sleep because the Lord sustains me.

During this time of pandemic, many persons are having insomnia. They are disturbed and have difficulty sleeping because they do not know what the future holds. Perhaps they have lost their jobs, or their work hours have been drastically reduced or they are furloughed. Perhaps they are unable to get to the store to pick up food for themselves and their family. Perhaps they are distraught because they or a loved one has come down with the Coronavirus. But I am reminded, and I remind you that the psalmist says, I lie down and sleep because the Lord sustains me. These simple words assure us that God will sustain us, even when we sleep. I know saying it is easy to sleep would be futile. But, God wants us to remember to say your prayers as children often do when we go to bed, and to be reminded that God will sustain us. And so that little prayer, "I lay me down to sleep, I pray the Lord my soul to keep, If I should die before I wake, I pray the Lord my soul to take." We all need to find comfort in those simple words and comfort in the words of the Psalmist when he says I lie down and sleep. I wake again because the Lord sustains me.

So, if you have been having trouble sleeping because the world looks like it's in the midst of a nightmare, or if you have been having trials and tribulations in your life and find difficulty to be at rest and peace, remember these words, God sustains us. So go forth from this place, knowing that the God who made us will also sustain us. God Remember us when we sleep. Give us peace of mind and clarity of heart, remind us, O, God, that you will sustain us and that you care for us. Therefore, we can sleep peacefully knowing that we are in your hands. Amen.

Day 33

Prayer: Merciful God, we come to you today with supplication and thanksgiving requesting that you will give to us the peace which passes all human understanding.

Scripture: "Do not worry about anything, but in everything by prayer and supplication with thanksgiving let your requests be made known to God. And the peace of God, which surpasses all understanding, will guard your hearts and minds in Christ Jesus. Philippians 4:6-7

Reflection: During these times of pandemic, there's conflict between the federal and the state governments. There's conflict between countries regarding how we ought to respond to the Covid 19 virus. And in the midst of these trying situations, many of us have become anxious and worried. But the author of Philippians says that we should not worry. Perhaps, you are saying that is easy for him to say. He does not have to deal with all of the strife and toils that we deal with.

From the beginning of time, trials always have been part of the human situation. The author of Philippians knows about trials and tribulations and persecution. He's not saying that life does not have problems. But he is saying in the midst of the problems of life, we should not worry, because we have a peace that passes all human understanding. And that peace is found through our Lord and Savior, Jesus Christ. The author of Philippians said, Whenever you find yourself worried, whenever you find yourself feeling overwhelmed, pray to Jesus Christ, Christ will hear our prayers, our cries will bring about a change in our lives.

Our message today is one that appears to be simple, but one that is often difficult for us to do. It is a challenge that whenever we find ourselves worried, anxious, and overwhelmed, to go to the Lord in prayer, and God will give us peace. It may not solve the problem right then at that very moment, but we'll have a peace that passes all human understanding, a peace of knowing that God is still in charge, sitting high on the throne, and that God will be there with us and for us. And so, my parting words for us today are do not worry about anything. But in everything by prayer and supplication with thanksgiving, make our requests known to the Almighty Amen, amen, and amen.

Day 34

Prayer: Almighty and everlasting God teach us how to stand firm on the solid rock of Jesus Christ. Teach us in spite of challenges of life, to hold on to your unchanging hands. Be with these your people. Be with us, God, during this time. Teach us to remember that we are your people, and that you will always be with us, and we can stand firm. In thy name, amen.

Scripture: Therefore, my brothers and sisters, whom I love and long for, my joy and crown, stand firm in the Lord in this way, my beloved. Philippians 4:1

Reflection: During these times, in almost any time in life when we have trials and tribulations and struggles, we want to run away. But God is reminding us to stand firm. The author of Philippians is saying that trials and difficulties will come in our lives. But God wants us to remain firm. The author of Philippians says stand firm in the Lord at all times.

Our challenge today is that we should stand firm in the Lord, regardless of all of the trials and tribulations that come our way. In spite of the pandemic Coronavirus, Covid 19 and the economic situations that we face, God wants us to stand firm. So, I challenge us today to remember who we are and whose we are. We are people called and set aside by God, not to become overly anxious or worried, but instead to remain firm and stand firm on the solid ground because we stand firm on the solid rock known as Jesus Christ. And, so, whenever we are challenged, whenever we are fearful, whenever we are anxious or nervous, remember these words to stand firm on the solid rock. "On Christ, the solid rock I stand, all other ground is sinking sand."

Day 35

Prayer: Lord, we come today with trials, tribulations, anxieties, and worries. Remind us that Jesus said, "Do not worry about tomorrow." So let us release our anxieties and our fears. And let us turn them over to you, dear God, knowing that you hear our prayers, and that you will answer our prayers. In Thy name and in the name of Jesus Christ. Amen.

Scripture: So, do not worry about tomorrow, for tomorrow will bring worries of its own. Today's trouble is enough for today. Matthew 6:34

Reflection: Our emphasis today is on how often we worry about so many things in life. We worry about what tomorrow might bring. But in Matthew, the sixth chapter, Jesus is reminding us that we should not worry about tomorrow. For tomorrow will have enough troubles of its own. Each day has its own trials and tribulations in the midst of this pandemic, and in the midst of this situation in which we find ourselves. God is reminding us through these words of Jesus that we should not worry.

Perhaps you feel like saying, well, that's easy for you to say. But remember, Jesus also had many things to worry about. He was faced with worry about rejection from his own people, worries of being tempted by the devil, worries about being beaten, spit upon, crucified and buried in a borrowed grave. In spite of all of the difficulties of life and the worries and trials that he would have to undergo, Jesus knew he could go to the Lord in prayer.

Jesus reminds us today that even though we may have trials, tribulations, and anxieties, we don't know what tomorrow holds. And many of us are fearful and nervous about the pandemic and about the economic situation that we find ourselves in. God wants us to take a deep breath in and breathe out. Jesus is reminding us of these words, do not worry about tomorrow. These words are very powerful. For many, they make no logical sense. For some, they may be irrational. But as Christians, we believe in the word of God and the words of Jesus Christ His Son. And Jesus wants us to be reminded that he is there for us and will take care of us. There is no problem too large for God to handle. Let us take our burdens to the Lord and leave them there.

In the Chapel there is a chancel rail. Sometimes in the middle of the day, I come over and I kneel down and pray when I feel burdened. I invite you in your homes or wherever you are to kneel down and pray. Take your worries and burdens to the Lord and leave them there.

Day 36

Prayer: Dear God, we come now in prayer, putting our trust in you and in your presence.

Scripture: Trust in the Lord with all your heart, and do not rely on your own insight. In all your ways acknowledge Him, and He will make straight your paths. Proverbs 3:5-6

Reflection: When I was younger and I had just graduated from college, I often thought I knew many things. I graduated with honors from Tugaloo College, and I thought that I was well-versed and knowledgeable about many things, particularly in my field of endeavor, political science. I then obtained a master's degree from Ole Miss and thought that I knew even more. But as life would have it, the older I get, and the more experiences I have, the less I have begun to trust in my own understanding, and my own knowledge. Perhaps some of you are the same way. It makes no difference how academically accomplished we are if our hearts and souls are not aligned and in sync with God.

We need to trust ultimately in Almighty God. So often, during times of crisis, we try to solve our problems by ourselves. We attempt to equate our human understanding with God's great wisdom. But God is the One who created us. There is nothing wrong with human knowledge. But we need to be reminded that it comes from Almighty God, and that we must turn to God during all situations, particularly in times like these. We should trust not in our own human understanding, especially during this time of pandemic, this time of trial and tribulation, but rather we should put our trust in God. God will see us through this. We are not alone. God will make our path straight. God will continually be with us. For those of us who feel alone and think we have to figure everything out so we can be at peace, we can put our hope and faith and trust in Almighty God. I invite you to do the same today, tomorrow, and forever, amen!

_____

_____

_____

_____

_____

_____

_____

Day 37

Prayer: God, feed us with your Holy Spirit. We are your children, and you love us. You care for us and protect us. You created us in your image to serve you. In thy name, amen.

Scripture: People were bringing little children to him in order that he might touch them; and the disciples spoke sternly to them. But when Jesus saw this, he was indignant and said to them, "Let the little children come to me; do not stop them; for it is to such as these that the kingdom of God belongs. Truly I tell you, whoever does not receive the kingdom of God as a little child will never enter it." And he took them up in his arms, laid his hands on them, and blessed them. Mark 10:13-16

Reflection: The other day at staff meeting, I mentioned that I missed seeing the little children at the church. We have a preschool and a nursery. I have come to know many of these little children by name. There is big Jack and a little Jack. There is a Caroline, I could go on and on with a list of names. I love the children and I miss them dearly. I mentioned that I loved sitting down with them during lunch and having conversation with them, and that I miss them sharing their candy with me (lol). The next day, I looked in my box in the office, and there was a bag of my favorite chocolate candy. That brought a smile to my face and to my mouth.

Perhaps your child or your children or grandchildren are suffering during this time. They cannot go to school. They cannot interact physically with their friends, playmates, and classmates. Perhaps they become despondent and are sad. I would like for you to remind them that even during these times, God is still with them and with us. And God does love them. Recently, we had a Facebook message from our youngest granddaughter. She was relaxing in a box outside just looking up at the sky. I was reminded that children are God's special creation, and that God will not allow them to suffer. And so those of you who are parents and grandparents, those of you who miss the little children as I do, know that Jesus loves the little children and, therefore, they will not be punished. God, we pray that You will Come now, touch the little children touch, the parents, and grandparents. Remind all of us that one day soon we will gather again. Amen.

Day 38

Prayer: Dear God, the past can, and often does, cause us great discomfort. Open us to be able to receive your words of love and forgiveness, we pray in Your name.

Scripture: The Lord says, "Forget the former things, do not dwell on the past. See, I am doing a new thing."   Isaiah 43:18-19

Reflection: These words, perhaps, for some of us can be troubling. For the Lord says, "Forget the former things, do not dwell on the past. See, I am doing a new thing." I recently wrote a letter to the staff at the church. In that letter, I talked about how things, in my opinion, would never ever be the same, that we can remember fondly the way things used to be. Here is an example: I was watching the NFL draft the other evening, and I was saddened that the players were not able to gather in the same room as their names were called by the NFL Commissioner. I wondered how long it would be before the National Football League play resumes and I would be able to cheer for my favorite players and teams. It brought sadness to my heart. Then I read these words, "Forget the former things and do not dwell on the past."

So often, we get bogged down in the way things used to be, so much that we cannot move forward. It does not mean that we do not commemorate and celebrate those things that have occurred in the past. But it means, rather, that God wants us not to get stuck in the past, but to live in the present and move toward the future. You perhaps, like me, are sad that life is not anything like it used to be. This Covid virus is not like anything we had imagined. God wants us to know that we are living in the present. God is reminding us that God is with us in all circumstances. That God, in the midst what seems to be a troubling and overwhelming situation, is creating something new.

I do not know what tomorrow brings, none of us do. But I know who holds tomorrow in His hands. And it is God Almighty. Our challenge today, is to look to the future, to live in the present, and to prepare for tomorrow. And that might mean living and worshiping differently than we've ever done before. I thank God for technology. I thank God for people who can reach out to others through long distances. And perhaps it might mean that we have church differently than we have ever before.

Our youngest daughter is graduating from Mississippi State this May. The graduation will not be anything like we had expected. We will not be able to gather and to celebrate her great accomplishment as we had expected. In the midst of it all, God is creating a new thing and that somehow, some way, everything will be okay. So let us not get stuck in the past, but rather let us look to the future, remembering that God is with us.

Day 39

Prayer: Lord, hear our prayer today as we seek your wisdom and guidance during this time of pandemic.

Scripture: Strengthen your feeble arms and weak knees, make level paths for your feet, so that the lame may not be disabled, but rather healed. Hebrews 12:12-13

Reflection: What powerful words the author of Hebrews is sharing with us. We live in a time where people feel weak, when people feel disabled, where people feel perhaps that life will never ever be the same. We feel disembodied. But the author of Hebrews is telling us that we all need to strengthen our weak arms, our feeble arms, and our weak knees. The author of Hebrews is reminding us that we are not a weak people, that we are a strong people, for we have been made by an almighty God, and God will be with us and strengthen us.

Our challenge today is to stand up during the trials that we are facing, in the midst of the pandemic, in the midst of the shortages, in the midst of all that is seemingly overwhelming us. God is reminding us through the author of Hebrews, that we need to stand firm, strengthen our arms, strengthen our knees, stand up straight and tall as our mothers used to say. For we have a God who will never ever leave us alone. The lame will be healed. And the difficulties of life that we are now facing will pass. God is with us. God will never ever be isolated from us.

I say to you today, in the words of the author of Hebrews, "Strengthen your feeble arms and your weak knees." Stand firm and stand tall and the word of God because we are God's people. And as God's people, we are not alone. Amen, amen and amen.

Day 40

Prayer: God, touch us, fill us with your spirit. God you are the beginning and the end, the Alpha, and the Omega, that without you there are no others. We ask and pray to you, O God, that you would strengthen and guide us and allow us to be receptive to your word this day. In thy name, amen.

Scripture: I am the Alpha and the Omega, the beginning, and the end, to the thirsty, I will give water without cost from the spring of the water of life. Revelation 21:6

Reflection: This brief scripture reminds us that God is omnipotent. God is omnipresent. God is the beginning and the end. In the Greek alphabet, Alpha is the first letter and Omega, the last letter. We are reminded, according to the author of Revelation, that God was there from the beginning, and God will be there at the end. God always has been and always will be with us. Those of us who are human beings are reminded by this passage of scripture that God will provide for us. The One who was there at the beginning, will be there at the end of human history.

In the meantime, it also says that God will provide water. Water is the source of life. God is the provider of all that we need — food, water, shelter, companionship — God provides it all. This passage of scripture from the last book of Revelation reminds us that God is omnipresent. He's everywhere. God is omnipotent. He is all powerful. And so those of us who are called by his name, need not worry or fear, or be anxious, because the Almighty God will provide for us. And so, during this time of trial and tribulation, during this time of anxiety and isolation, we are reminded that we serve a powerful God, the only God, and that God will provide for us and take care of all our needs.

About The Author

Rev. Dr. Embra Jackson Jr. is the Senior Pastor of First United Methodist Church, Tupelo, Mississippi. Prior to this appointment, he had been the District Superintendent of the Starkville District since 2011. He served as the Administrative Assistant to Bishop Hope Morgan Ward from 2005 to 2011.

Rev. Dr. Jackson graduated in 1974, Cum Laude from Tugaloo College (Jackson, MS) with a bachelor's degree in Political Science; in 1979, he earned a Master of Public Administration from the University of Mississippi (Oxford, MS); in 1985 he received a M. DIV. from the Interdenominational Theological Center (Atlanta, GA). In 1992, he received a teacher's certification from Mississippi State University. In addition, in 2003, he received a Doctor of Ministry (D. Min) from Memphis Theological Seminary.

Rev. Dr. Jackson has served as pastor to Holmes County Larger Parish of the UMC; Kosciusko Wesley UM Charge; Griffin UMC; St. Paul UMC, West Point, MS; Central UMC, Jackson, MS; and Aldersgate UMC, Jackson, MS. He has been the Executive Director of the United Methodist Metro Ministers, Jackson, MS; Chaplain of Hospice Ministries, Inc., Ridgeland, MS; Instructor at Wood College; and as a teacher in the Starkville Public Schools.

Embra possesses an ecclesiastical endorsement from The Board of Higher Education and Ministry. He is a Certified Coach in the International Coach Federation and CoachNet and currently a Spiritual Leadership Institute Apprentice.

Rev. Dr. Jackson and his wife, Rosia are parents to four adult children.

Rev. Dr. Embra Jackson and his wife Rosia Jackson

Rev. Dr. Embra Jackson Jr.

www.ingramcontent.com/pod-product-compliance
Lightning Source LLC
Chambersburg PA
CBHW081754100526
44592CB00015B/2426